For Yuri, Gabe and Anna

All Day, All Night

CATH KENNEALLY lives in Adelaide, South Australia, and makes radio programs on Australian arts and literature. Her collections to date include *Harmers Haven* (1996) and *Around Here* (1999). Her first novel, *Room Temperature*, appeared 2000. she has won a Barbara Hanrahan Fellowship, Adelaide Festival of Arts 1998, and John Bray National Poetry Prize for *Around Here*, Adelaide Festival 2002. *All Day All Night* has been shortlisted for Vincent Buckley Poetry Prize. She has three children.

All Day, All Night

CATH KENNEALLY

SALT

PUBLISHED BY SALT PUBLISHING
PO Box 937, Great Wilbraham, Cambridge PDO CB1 5JX United Kingdom
PO Box 202, Applecross, Western Australia 6153

First published 2003

Printed and bound in the United Kingdom by Lightning Source

Typeset in Swift 9.5 / 13

ISBN 1 876857 09 9 paperback

SP

1 3 5 7 9 8 6 4 2

Contents

Acknowledgments

Some of these poems have appeared in the following anthologies and journals: *Atlantic Review* (USA), *Southerly*, *Otis Rush*, *Heat*, *Hobo*, *Overland*, *Meanjin*, *Forked Tongues*, *Eat the Ocean*, *JAAM* (NZ), *Sport* (NZ), *Landfall* (NZ), and broadcast on *Poetica* (ABC Radio National) and 5UV Radio Adelaide.

Sister Wendy

friend to the world, roving
art critic for the BBC

she spends seven hours
a day in prayer, only two at work
    (naturally some smartarse saint
    once said work *was* prayer)

two Ryvitas a day, a pint of skim, she
lives in a trailer in the Anglian woods

enthusing at an art show, she was
snapped up by a Beeb TV crew
waiting to film Greer

    now she travels the globe, seeing her beloved pictures
    for the first time, a miniature Kenneth Clark in wimple
    and specs, burbling unscripted for the camera

unworldly, unprudish as well, an overnight byword
for exclaiming over 'lovely, fluffy' pubic hair
on a Stanley Spencer nude

up before the lark, coffee and prayers,
penance for things she's never done, or
pure *carpe diem* zing

she has no faith, she jokes, she's never known doubt
handing over to Rev. Mother at 16, silence and cunning
enough to win a stash of Oxford prizes

'It's been so easy, I have to laugh' – and I agree
the call so clear, the way so straight, encumbrances
so obvious for what they were

one day, she'll evaporate like woodland mist
weightless and resolved, unified and true
leaving us thrashing in our ephemera

the art-show fluke a *felix culpa* for us, if not for her
an innocent abroad at 66 – God sentences her to
martyrdom by exposure

Poem for Linda

my right breast hurts
hurts to touch and even
when I leave it alone

which is worrying. Were you here
when I had it checked
early this year?

they said not a lump
more a corrugation, and
come back straight after

your next period, but
I never did

You sent me a poem once
about dangerous breasts
by Kate Llewellyn (?)

All day I feel as if I've got
packets of explosives
taped to my ribs, till

the breast stops hurting
and I take refuge in
the notion that it's

just hormonal, like
this bloated stomach

Lately, you sent me
a poem of your own

about Dracula's mother
suckling her monster..

asking, (in brief), when he died
did she still feel something?

very you, that poem:
playing with Gothic,

held in check by your
own brand of irony

I miss your equilibrium
tower of strength that you are

in future I foresee you
being less strong

your poem says you realise
how much mothering
of intractable creatures

you've done to date
and might just stop

Dare to Swim

Bea rings me
after years

she liked my
radioed poem

updates me
on the struggle

hers, ours, tho
hard to mean 'ours'

when our humil-
iations are so

minutely particular
and shameful

they echo unsaid while
    we talk up big

            Bea talks saving
            Christies Creek

    she and her cronies
    spit bitcheries at
    Council goons in
    cement-trucks

    who want concrete runnels
    to flush offending fluids

    would shove frogmouth females
    in while they're at it

    wash them out to sea

if their men can't shut them up

some offer to shut Bea up
with a well-placed fist

Ed's left home because she's rude
resists correction (fists, well-meant)

we talk up tough but the runoff
sweeps us up, sharp scree stings

  I hear Bea singing
  years ago

  our Honours do
  guitars and carols

  carols seem silly now
  in all this water

At night, Bea departs the public fray
for the home front

the new quiet of her sealed house
filling up fast with backwash

she paddles like Mao in the Yangtze
game but strapped for breath

riding the rips, singing
snatches of marching-songs

in the lulls; nearly sure
she'd sooner swim

than swear we're
on dry land

The Visitation

As of now, two of us in my house
need 'sanitary protection'

Anna is second, after her friend Caroline
to 'get them', in sixth class

    here come forty years of hormonal
    dictatorship

    a red line drawn under gender-neutral
    childhood

    disposal problems, flash-floods,
    crazed compulsion to wear white
    on first days

    family folk-wisdom (my mother's side)
    forbids first-day baths
    and hair-washing

        schoolyard jargon used to have it that
        on 'those' days, 'Aunt Agatha' was 'visiting'
        in her red sports car

        As Anna and I choose pads at the chemist's
        I'm visited by an image of my mother
        on her knees in our Housing Trust toilet

        helping me loop pad-ends through
        the teeth of a 'sanitary belt'

        the floor is cold, polished concrete
        we slide the deplenished green and white pack
        in between the water-heater and the wall

out of sight of uninitiated siblings
a comradely moment

the date is August 15th, Feast of the Assumption, a Big Day
in the Catholic calendar, marked by a special school concert

that evening, I'm waiting to read a poem when I discover,
finally, the long-awaited evidence of womanhood
in the toilets, just before the curtain

I'm fourteen and a half. When we get home, Mum
shows me the ropes, secretly, in the loo

Anna, at twelve, is sufficiently composed
to wear a pad to school on her first day
on her own initiative

lets me in on her news only later
in the car, as we drive home

no incinerators, these days, in girls' toilets
acrid smell of smouldering bandages
at home time, after long afternoon classes

called 'periods' – the classes and the menses

the nuns bled discreetly
under white serge

we imagined boxes and boxes of Modess
stacked in high cloister cupboards

If Mary was immaculate, did
Aunt Agatha come to visit?
Did we ever ask?

IC

I remember Dad, when I was eight or so,
just home from his milkround,
at the breakfast-table with Mum,
crying, because his mother had died
in the night

Nanna had burned away alarmingly fast
to a bony doll. We went to see her
in the narrow bed at Kath's house

I remember this as we stand, crying, around
Dad's bed. He hasn't shrunk, he just
looks himself, his healthiest self

but they tell us he won't hang on long
and we have to believe them

Just lately he told me he never felt free enough
with his own father, old Con, to call him 'Dad'
he called him 'Father' till the day he died

the nurses in Intensive Care are 'marvellous'
we all keep saying this for two days
while Dad lies there

till Des, the last of us, arrives from Melbourne
The brisk consultant sweeps in to whip away
the tubes, with the help of the marvellous nurse

we watch Dad's face, the monitor, his face
the purple heartbeat line on the screen
continues to register
a few minutes more
then drops out

alive, helpless, we keep on crying
the marvellous nurse and doctor
leave us alone

Be Where, Now?

often I'm troubled by visions
of the splendid houses of friends
who live elsewhere

like Greg and Jen's house
clinging to its Hataitai hillside . . .

where best to be
where waking there
would be a comfort?

In Melbourne, perhaps the home
of my dreams, I meet Mary Kenneally
a saint of our days

saintly an unaccustomed word
that I reach for nonetheless

people sense her attending to them
a skill only saints have

recently ill, she is frail
thin, her straight black hair veil-like
each side of her pale, luminous face

fragile and intense, like Catherine
(of Siena), harrier of Popes, woman
Doctor of the Church (one of only two:
she and Teresa of the transfixed heart)

I meet her 96-year-old uncle
when we go to hear a lecture
from Tim Pat Coogan, rebel Irish historian

we diaspora'd Irish fill the college hall
pass round icecream containers
to raise Tim Pat's fare to Sydney

Mary's uncle smiles and smiles
in overcoat, vest and tie. He is, you'd say,
seventy at the outside. Are these my people?

My fraught three days in Eire were
not conclusive, yet every person on the street
was the spit of someone I was at school with

Our name, hers and mine, means
 Head of the Wolf

She launches a book called *Wee Girls*, the day
we meet, Irish women's tales from home and away

Her Irish fervour is new, but ardent
a Famine Remembrance Committee one of her works

I scratch at earth thinly-raked across these buried questions
Catholic Irish Irish Catholic Irish . . .

No, God's gone for good
for the other, my heart still catches

I find myself telling these people my name
as though reciting a password

Eureka

Across from Manta Cafe in Norwood
is Emulation Masonic Hall

an anagrammatist's delight: recast, it's
Emasculation on a Hill – and there's been

blood in the foyer, in fact, at Parliament House
this week, as Aboriginal protesters storm the doors

howls of outrage in the Press, apologies all round
where are the shouts of acclaim?

our dusty Renault windows still sport Eureka flags
but we're a sorry lot

out on the Norwood streets today
two well-away mad boys

one in a hooded Policeman Plod cape
tall, ferret-faced, prowling behind

an unsuspecting girl, raising himself up
on his toes, lifting his arms high

as if to whisk her, Boris Karloff style,
into his cloak, a vampire swipe

he even laughs that way, hoo hoo, hoo hoo
to himself, not too loud

another boy walks a kind of ghost walk
back and shoulders rigid, arms clenched

clutching the hem of his shirt
legs gripped tight together

moving visibly only at the knees
eyes like saucers, he wishes

not to be here. Thank you, they say
we'll find our own way out

'Be Cheerful, Richmond'

Richard 111, Act V Sc. iii

at the bend of the Yarra
by the Skipping Girl sign
it's tranquil as Tuscany
if you stand on the bridge
facing upstream, away from
the factories, though these
from the back are not
unpicturesque
ignore the joggers &
cyclists, there's a river-
meadow down there
to the left, vines growing
morning light glistening
on poplars
green on green on green
Victoria Street, all the same
just a few steps away
my route back to Pete &
Helen's, past skipping girl,
playground with plastic
rubbish bags, Schizophrenia
Can be Cured billboard
Vital Youth Victoria's
fascist-looking grasped-hands
symbol, the Johnny Young
Talent School, the Vietnamese
shops, Peter Jackson carton $36
Unsilence the Lambs : Operation
Paradox, a skittled stop-light
my shocking posture revealed
in a shopfront window
Church Street Vietnamese
temple, dozens of tiny balloons
over the doorway, six pairs

of shoes on the step
Laity Street Sunday morning
verandah with two companionable
armchairs either side of
a baby's carseat
Little Kent, Buckingham,
Somerset, Richmond . . .
it's the cast of *Richard the Third*
yet the residents are mostly
Asian, all kinds
out of sight
a large wimpy dog
whining itself hoarse

Little Corporal

video tea-break
freeze-frame
Prime Suspect 4
behind the great
pinched little face
of Helen Mirren
who frowns
in concentration
a WPO in grey
T-shirt, butch,
beautiful, chopped
grey hair, determined
jaw, striding between
the male coppers
all looking elsewhere
she never appears
again
Helen has slipped
one hand inside
the top flap
of her shirt
Napoleon-style
for some reason
a terribly
affecting gesture

O Lucky Man

doesn't it kill you the way
they sew little bows onto
women's undies

as if every time you
put on a bra and knickers
you were gift-wrapping presents

Beach Dream

I'm trying to reclaim a small, indeed a dwarf dressing-table
being washed into shore, the tide almost having reached
the sea wall, the waves pushing the dresser further and further
to the right of me. From the shore, I try to follow its progress
but I'm being trapped by the incoming tide. Just as I reach over
to lay a hand on the floating miniature, I find myself at a turn in
    the wall, and my
feet disappear from under me as the wash surges
round the corner, where it's much deeper. I struggle out of the sea
make a few more swipes at my quarry which has retreated
way out of reach again. So I give up and go to my clothes
(I'm not wearing any) further up the beach, since now
it's dark, and the esplanade lights are coming on

Fair Cop

Tiny, jewel tragedies
sit winking in the past
minute on any global scale
yet compact, all the same
of pressurised sadness

a story found its way to me
returned from weeks in Europe
how a friend found my six-year-old
(left behind) sitting, as he thought
unobserved, on a doorstep
crying quietly to himself

hot coals heaped on my head
that haven't cooled in all this time
a guilty, impotent grief. It still seems
the seeds of every later pain
lie there, in that moment
of my absence

Six Years Gone

I'd like to see you
    walking down the street
sometimes I think I do

        hint of a swagger in the stride
    bit of a frown,
        charming, but, as always

long legs with those
            unexpectedly wide
        Wilkinson-men hips

I could pull the car over
        to the side of the road,
            you could slide into
                    the passenger-seat

I would take you wherever you were going
we could catch up, Pat, old son

        what d'you say?

An Irish Reel

An Irish reel that's always been a favorite
on the Lucky Oceans radio show
Lucky reminds us it's called 'Old Hag,
You Have Killed Me', and with that
I receive an image of dark-shawled women
walking two paces behind their men
they still do in parts of rural Ireland
a country, too, where girls and boys
are segregated, and for longer, than
in most others

Back in the wide brown place,
Honest John, our Baby Boss, decrees
by magisterial sulk that here there shall be
no more 'chairperson', no 'him or her', but
'he' and 'his' shall be heard once more
in the land, and only 'he'
– all contracts to be signed
by the Man in Charge, boyo!

Yet an Irish reel still sets me mentally
going through my paces, sometimes my feet,
too – Irish Dancing medals gather dust
at home – our flying girl-child feet
on concert-hall boards were liberated
by the forms they learned
we were lifted up, we believed
we belonged to that soulful band
our dresses with their brief green capes
mimicked the priests' own robes

Just this morning, we hear on JJJ
two of the young activists at the tent city
behind the NSW parliament. One is Kitty
O'Gorman, the other is Peter O'Brien,
begorrah!

Battered Irish stereotypes I can't let go
a populace outraged by oppression
(not only their own), crafters of beauty
in words and music, crafty, too
Gerry Adams begins a magazine chat
with a reference to Yeats ('too much sacrifice
makes of the heart a stone'), and I warm,
comrade-like, to Yeats, the old fraud
and the way Adams has him
at his fingertips

Whubarb, Whubarb

a rude, protracted motorbike raspberry
overrides the mellifluous accents of Adams, as
Phillip and his guest debate European unity

Professor William Someone has ludicrous
difficulties with his 'r's. He says 'Fwanco-
Amewican' so distinctly it's Pythonesque

Doctor Hans Someone warns that half
a century of history cannot be put away
in less than a decade, even though Blair

is a 'bright young perky politician'. Adams
chips in with 'I was having dinner tonight
with an ex-Prime Minister of this country'

I tune out about the time William, whom
I'm now thinking of as 'Welease Woger'
enunciates 'pwimawily for political weasons'

enough of this, as a day of eggshell-walking
ends, of collecting forces and girding loins
shaky ground underfoot, firm till now

as I take in the fact my mother's illness
won't go away, there's a time-limit
to how long she can fight it

her daughters are suddenly infirm ourselves
at the thought of her going. It's
not, in fact, thinkable

though Adams is quizzing his next guest
on death and embalming – his old
hobby-horse. I rather hope

dying will scare the pants off Phillip
how can he not want his mother around
for ever, like the rest of us?

Olwyn's Place

(Hindmarsh Island)

Sandwiched in the canoe
between layers of sky
and water
still, glassy channel
honey-coloured in the sunset
suspended feeling of being held
high in mid-air
sky flattened above
water endless below

no speedboats, the odd pelican
reeds and sandhills to one side
jetties and shacks on the other
a family of humans cavorting
at high tide by their boat ramp
Gabe and I rowing in reasonable synch
down towards Goolwa
away from the Mouth

Each of these days sees
Anna Bea Lucy Lisa
'mudding' together
the fun more strenuous
on the day Corin leaves
the girls' screams
hysteria-edged, that
yesterday were merely hilarious
a hormonal wildcard queering the pack

Trackies wet across the beam
from the paddle over
dillybags, sunscreen, floppy hats
boots for the mud, a last-day
Coorong walk. On the ocean side

we collect plastic bags and rubbish
as well as shells,
subside at the foot of a dune to
drink thermos coffee
lament four-wheel-drive tracks
stretching into the spray-
misted distance

Si Peu

comme il y a si peu de temps
since there is so little time
I must attend very soon to
lilies and roses and olives
in the front garden
someone is calling
morning! morning!
two women
across the road
chattering in a
European language
comme il y a
si peu
as there is so little
sunshine here
we must make
the most of it
and of the chances
we are offered
not always so
easy to recognise
and how best to
use the time
which slips away
comme il y a si peu
so we could sit
on the veranda
soak up sun
make contact
with someone
call our brother
to arrange
to have coffee
read what
someone else
has made

of their *si peu de*
time, talent
the sun seems
central to all this
by no means
enough in a
lifetime, only
enough to be
going on with
illumination,
warmth
trams here
are plentiful
my brother
has an Irish joke
about a potato clock
the doormat
is fraying
the lily leaves
are strong, defiant
an old friend
of my brother's
lives just across
the road
from here
Tom himself
lives, amazingly
around the corner
il y a si peu
there are so few
mais aujourd'hui
il fait beau
two people with
funny yet practical
hats go by
one has a
fluffy moustache
forget-me-nots

and violets
by the gate
a picket fence
roses not quite
in bloom
flats and chimneys
Unit 4 For Sale
Tom wants to
go to Japan
and to visit
Juan Davila
who lives nearby
Tom is collecting
junk metal and
clock parts
for a skull sculpture
he's found a
dentist's model
of a jaw, left
in someone's garden
growing tendrils
a Tam o'Shanter
jaunty on a head
in the theatre
yesterday covered
chemo-baldness
comme les jours
sont si peu
as there are so few
days
should we gather
our children round
us now, attempt
to pass on
such wisdom
as we have gained
comme nous avons
si peu de mots

as so few words
make any difference
Auden says
dance while you can
to lose all sense
of urgency
is wise, perhaps
comme nous sommes
si peu nombreux
as we are so few
a huge silver
number 9
flaking back
to black
on the house
of Tom's friend
il y a si peu de gestes
there are but few
signs we can make
but make them
make them
tonight going to
an Irish rally
perhaps to connect
comme il faut
as you must
as you do

Millennial Two-Step

armaggeddon
Elmore Leonard
hallelujah
Andy Warhol
discourse theory
Willa Cather
techno-wizard
okanuis
Ella Baché
superhighway
Kingsley Amis
Intifada
Oprah Winfrey
weight loss clinics
García Marquez
fibre-optics
Roy and HG
condominiums
Geoffrey Archer

Globetrot

travelling in dream cities
forced to take ship
from a stinking squalid quayside
amid soaring tangles of
spars and gantries
deposited here by bus
cold and rained-on
everything grey and grimy
waiting to board by
rusting rail lines
God knows where this is
an enormous, anonymous port

speeding against the clock
to make a rendezvous
in a town like Hobart
hilly, sunlit timber houses
lost, now, on a construction site
preponderance of yellows
in the cityscape
challenged roughly by some man
I push my way out
through a loose paling
into a familiar-looking,
precipitous street

short of time in London
I've promised to visit old friends
but other engagements take me
to a distant part of the city
where I wander about
an imposing Palladian building
a cultural centre, a conservatorium
I meet a group of people
on the grand front steps
we go to see a film

Sydney, and once more embarrassed
by my double-booking habit
no time to phone, I turn up unannounced
my friends are astonished to see me
they're on their way somewhere
oh dear, I fly out tomorrow
we'll catch up over breakfast
by the water somewhere
D elegant as ever,
M superbly cool

Round One

shadow-boxing all day
waking retake of a small-hours round

        old assailants *redivivus*
        bright new monsters
        sprung full-formed

one of those dreams where you lose the lot

so engulfing that you inhabit your
castaway state for ten waking minutes

all day fling hunted glances
over the shoulder

        probe the tender spot
            where a piece of psyche
                    like a hammered thumb
                            works to repair itself

this is how we rehearse for griefs-in-waiting

even though, when they descend
they drop silent as doodlebugs

    reduce your house to rubble
    suck all the air out of your lungs

        a tiny part of you whispers
        yep, been here before

Buongiorno

Cafe Buongiorno noise, fragmented, constant
        grey holiday outside
            a kid on top note

my Sara Paretsky novel, despite Kathleen Turner
    in the PI mugshot, grey also

        a blanket mood – when you look out
    from under it

        everything seems inexplicable

    three red cars bottleneck outside the parking lot

    tinny drums on the sound loop

        girls in skivvies and wide leg pants

        sundry saddish sale signs

        a man in a pirate headscarf
 a swirl of red braid on a bias-cut full circle black skirt

    why can't this be Melbourne?

two bulky middle aged women, matching short soft perms
heads together over tea

three serious Italian girls leaving the next table

If Gabe 'n the guys sailed in now from Surf 'n Ski next door
I'd have us halfway to the waves at Chinaman's
before they had time to ask

Hard Word

this month it's been that time
of month the whole month long

I walk with Linda round the Island
dead flat, miles and miles of sky

Bruni starts a hare. Later we both nurse
hot water bottles on the couch

back home, I plant time bombs
gypsophila and baby's breath

at a given signal, they'll rear up
I sit on the lawn, despite the damp

cross-legged, all my insides
dragged towards the centre of the earth

after all these years of hormone-rule
I can't distinguish chemical gloom

from true despair. The fish in the tank
burrowing under a favorite rock

seems to have it right. Until a spot
of blood explains my state of mind

and then the mood seems merely that
blessed relativity floods back

but universal dolour won't let go
without a final twitch

these regular morose annunciations
says a tiny voice, pave the way

for the real Hard Word
you wait

The Way Across

Baby Nina, impassive on her Nanna's knee
her one flash of vivacity over with stretching out
her arms, and a fleeting grin on sighting Moira
From the new perch she considers all of us
sitting on Jack's bed in the circle of lamplight
while it grows dark early beyond the venetians
She gravely shows us, when asked, her middle finger
where the reattached top joint looks red and sore
but is still there, not on the grass beside the
slammed shed door as it almost was four weeks ago
The day began warm but grew steel grey, rained
stayed absurdly mild, then snapped cold
with gloomy finality around half-one
What else is there to do but kid around
when one of us is sick and won't get well
it doesn't feel like avoiding the issue
we ask about drugs, and what they do
Jack and Moi both tell with equal zest
the story of the visiting house painter
quoting way too high, scared to death
when Jack tries to get out of his chair
finds his legs won't behave, and limp-falls
at the guy's feet (he's out the door in nanoseconds)
The drugs weaken muscles but keep him awake
The papers say legal euthanasia in the NT
would be by sedative followed by strong
muscle relaxant which would close down
lungs and heart. With the money not spent
on a new car, Moi and Jack are revamping
the rumpus room. We talk about our O/S trips
Jack and Moi alone amid a sea of alien French
billeted in Lourdes with a family who feed
and ignore them. They'd do it again, they say
and it's true, though most unlikely now
but that seems not the point
It's rained all night since then, and all today

I would have liked to spend the day in bed
then think of Jack who has to . . .
a Peter Bakowski poem recommends we look
at 'what you have done, what you have
mastered, and what you must do now'
a possible plan for one's last few days
if we're alert enough to live in them
Jack's mastered patience, forbearance,
plain speech plus kindness
an artesian flow of pride
in his kids, from a well of estimation
of what makes each tick, shrewdness
about how the world goes, magnanimity
of spirit, a great companionableness
and being present in his life. Now
he'll be wrapping up and channelling
intent, mentally sending what there is to send
'before scampering/ across the border/ like (a) bandit'

Black Rock

Brother wears a black cassock, black trousers
black shoes and socks,
black nuggets of rosary beads
slung on black leather belt

out behind the school, he's built a mini-railway
runs the single, tiny engine round the track
keeps it oiled, rides it once a month

down in the back paddock,
early in the school year
grasses collapsed and yellow
send my roots rain

the lads on the rugby field
grip each other's buttocks
sway together in a huddle

away in Newcastle,
down by the sea
another huddle of lads
ground a girl into the sand

Brother rides his engine,
blacks all that out
lulled by the rattle of the beads
the clack of the wheels

Note

Schoolgirl Lee Lee was raped and murdered by schoolboys at a party in Newcastle beach suburb Black Rock in 1983. The film of that name is by Neil Armfield.

Little Palindrome

Anna, little palindrome, my little/big girl as
you sign yourself

you write to tell me it's school holidays now
next term your last in Primary

Aaaarrggh! You say. And how! Next year
you march along to High School, third

in our line, last. Another rower, a girl
– hooray! Shoulders shaping up

You're strong, you tell me – and you are
at your age I was a weed

in second year, Mum taught me Latin
I hated it. Couldn't decide what to call her

so called her nothing. You can call
me 'bud', if it happens to you

(not likely). In this room, of Eleanor Dark's
– a novelist and a doctor's wife –

there's a set of Arthur Mee Children's Encyc-
lopaedias. Old. 'The Story of the Boundless

Universe and all its Wondrous Worlds'
'The Five Continents & 100 Nations & Races

That Inhabit Them'; 'Paul Saves Christianity'
'The League of Nations', 'Famous Modern Buildings'

and some Poetry: 'The Curfew Bell' ('Slowly England's
sun was setting o'er the hilltops far away')

you won't be getting much of England and her sun, or sons
Republic soon, and a new thousand years

though that means nothing, in this 'timeless land'
(that's what Eleanor Dark's novel's called)

I hope you travel, lots and lots, like a girl
who's here, called Jane, who's been all over

shows us photos of herself and dog, old station
-wagon, bedroll, campfire, tells us tales

I feel like a wuss, listening. Maybe we can
go outback together, in a few years' time

let's make a pact. When you finish school
we set off. Come back whenever. Whaddya say?

Mum

A Green Pen

a green pen, an environmentally friendly writing pad
Japanese students behind me on the bus, going
I guess to the College of English near my work

ebullient wattle in many front yards, while
back home Ken and Bob sit and go for walks
silent, or to the accompaniment of one of Bob's tales

which we'll all hear many times. A favorite, this visit
is the one about the enormously fat girl whom Bob
used to pick up, with others, in the firm car

'they gave me a new Holden every year' – she'd be
the last to deliver on the return trip from the new
Darrell Lea's – 'thirty mile trip' – so fat, in her

back seat corner, Bob, driving, was 'lookin' up at
the sky'; then the bit about her being born with eyes
sealed shut, having to be slit open, no lids, and the cop

pulling them over and saying 'Geez, Bob, what's that
you've got there?' I heard this one five times on Sunday
Today he's recovering from a full-length fall

at Port Adelaide yesterday. Maybe he remembers
how his nose came to be bruised and scabby,
maybe not, but he seems 'good, love'

Being Away

Being away
and being ill
I feel my way
to a decision:

all the garlic I can eat
or my lungs are history

a feeling too,
one breath at a time,
that small-time is all time
becomes a set
of resolutions:

I will wash salad leaves
slowly, one by one
under a gentle stream
of tap-water

I will hand-wash clothes
sometimes, or some things
every time, with
soft soap and rainwater

heavy things
will require strength
to wring and carry, wet
to hang out to dry

strength I don't have
quite yet, but soon

I will disassemble
the garden
sort it into bits
as they do here

bite-sized bits I shall
scale to suit my strength
and care for calmly
week by week
month by month

not considering the
economics of planting
vegetables. Just
planting them.
Looking around

this small town,
I see how it's done
what time of day
to stand among
the rows

a clamping pain
near the base of
my ribs, surprisingly fierce
not lungs but love

for my absent eldest, who
travelled to this country
with me, a wide-eyed ten,
ten years back. For him

I wish this calm
profusion – less admirably,
I wish it could be me
who gives it to him

Caro Diario

In the stone house
we wash clothes
in stream water
sit in the sun
when it's less
than ferocious
we drive around
serpentine roads
to lakes and towns
sit in the squares
with gelati
except Saturdays, when
boys go ape in *Api*
three-wheel baby vans
two-wheel spins
or hoon on Vespas
we sit in the house
out of the heat
read detective stories
eat mascarpone and
raspberries and tomatoes
let the days pass
kill scorpions at night
when they emerge
from the old timbers
in the ceiling
sleep sporadically
it stays hot upstairs
outside are chestnuts
figs and strawberries
lampuna bushes
mulberry trees
fireflies at dusk
wasps and butterflies
stinging nettles
and dock leaves

across the road
a cemetery mainly
occupied by Ferris &
Bertolinis
up the hill, the village
stone and cement
rural profound silence
intermittent growls of
a Ciclo round
the next corner
real woods, not forest
not bush
birds, not so many
as you'd think
dry leaves, mounds
of cut grass,
bees and blowflies
bracken, stone
retaining walls
wild yarrow
woodpiles
most Edenic, a green
snake, where I was
ready to put
my chair
Corin insists that
blatte are what you kill
with Blattox
(spray-can in kitchen)
what can they be?
little girl visits
Lisa's piano teacher
says her mother's gone
to buy a baby brother
but when he
comes home
she will *schiacciare*
him into the carpet

& hit him with a hammer
a cheering response
when all around
the churches are full
of lolly baby-Jesuses
latched crazily
onto anatomically-wrong
immaculate breasts
one unusual bas-relief
in Arezzo, 12 or 13 cent.
baby full length
on Mary's lap
her hands folded
on his swaddled chest
old, *dolce*, Joseph
stands guard to the side
remote angel extras
round the manger
this birth seems
an everyday miracle
another old man
today, at Gramolazzo lake
shows his grandson off
to his old friends
who drop their work
and fuss over him
for the next half hour
it's the wholly-family
ethos here

icons

the things that will acquire
heady nostalgia value

when we get back

sit ignored among the luggage

they are
Upim paper bags

Bei & Nannini sugar sachets

city *piante* for Pisa,
Perrugia, Arezzo

bus tickets used and unused

Garnier supermarket shampoo

a bra bought in Florence
in a tent behind a stall

Lines Idea sanitary pads

receipts, like this one, from

PROF. BINI E C SNC
VIA OBERDAN 10 PI
28/06/98

All Four Feet

Nothing neat. Nothing that lands on all four feet.
VIRGINIA WOOLF

and yet it's so tempting.
The Waves investigates
the need to 'make phrases'

sentences shored against the dark
willing the words to establish permanence
though the waves roll in and on and over

In this Julian Barnes book (patchy), there's
a part where three friends write their names
in the sand, and leap around, mock-furious

as the waves erase them when the tide comes in.
One, the intellectual, runs away up onto the pier
and sobs embarrassingly, uncontrollably

Virginia tries, in *The Waves*, to make
one character of-the-earth earthy, Lawrentian:
Susan, 'who says "I love. I hate"' – has babies

plants crops, strides around fields with men
points her stick at walls to be mended
gardens and cooks

not half as convincing as Jinny (fantasy-Virginia)
the social butterfly, who lives for the moment
has scads of men

or Bernard, the worrier, the sentence-maker,
the notetaker, whose self-styled 'footling' trip
to Rome is the extent of his travels, who

invents histories for strangers, who

has the last word, which is his account of how
his self, reliable, responsive to tiny stimuli

such as washing on clotheslines, someone sweeping
with a broom, this self has dissolved into immensity
his perceptions evaporating into nothing

because there are no stories, really, are there? And yet,
he's tolled back to his sole self by the hovering of the
waiter, the crumbs on the table, the grease on the knife

the waves broke on the shore, V writes, and you think
of water, waves and depths and the river stones
in the cardigan pocket

travelling fractures the shell, or case of self, as V says
you become *strana, étrangère*, you feel invisible, dispensable
not noteworthy, not a fact, just *viaggiante*, passing through

stand in the middle of a strange crowd, close your eyes
will you still be there when you open them again?
Like Virginia, whose book tells how finely alert she is

still as a mouse one day, still as a stone the next
I remember a fairy story which ends 'and the waves broke
over the two black stones' (who were once people)

the green outside this Tuscan window, beyond the shutters
is intense, immensely varied, planted and encouraged,
not wild: beanpoles and purple beans just feet away

several rows, one household's worth, ten paces long
two plum trees, parsley, lettuce, *pomodori*, fenced in
by another yield-bearing climber

I don't think the waves reach
this high up the mountain

Hello, Sailor

Biz said 'say hello to the boys in the Tuileries', but they'd moved
they were sunning themselves by the Seine alongside Pont Neuf
you could see them from the bus, glossy, all in a row
in tight boxer-shorts

From another bus in Firenze I leaned out of the window
to observe a boy in drag, at once discreet and outrageous
skin-tight jeans and little black top, shoulder bag no different
from those worn by many an Italian paterfamilias

the shimmy and the *moue*, the toss of head, discreet makeup
smart cropped curls were shocking amongst the Florentine
straights waiting to cross in one of the *haute-mode* hotspots
In Perugia tonight two boys in their thirties cut a swathe

through the seven o'clock promenade crowd, lean, absorbed,
graceful, dancers perhaps: narrow leather boots, black
dungarees, white tee shirt, one with cherry pink beanie rolled
back from seraphic *zingara* face, blue jeans, blue shirt

in Livignarno, Pat's father Hugo tells behind-the-hand tales
of lesbian folk singers in Perth, and, unaccountably, a bright
orange van trundles around the mountain corner, loudspeaker
lashed to the front of its cabin, squeaking a falsetto 'More' . . .

Hot Bitumen

Daniel and Marie-José open their house to us,
Australian visitors, friends of friends of theirs,
this anniversary-week in Caen
50 years since D-Day, the Normandy Landing,
Caen full of American tourists, the *grands magasins*
overflowing onto the pavements with
commemorative T-shirts, army fatigues,
camouflage caps, carry-bags with slogans:
Bienvenue Back Home in Normandy
Our hosts both teach – they lived
for seven years in Sydney,
the countryside – French specialists
for the Education Department.
They have many stories
which we hear over meals
(Marie-José and Daniel feed us
with great, though understated aplomb)
their first Australian country lunch invitation:
arriving expectant, they find their thongs-
and-shorts clad host dispensing beers from l'Esky,
not a sign of food of any kind. Without
warning, after half an hour or so, he leaps
aboard the Kingswood, waves cheerily,
disappears in a cloud of dust. Nonplussed,
they are attempting Gallic nonchalance
when host returns, laden with huge parcels
wrapped in newspaper. These he deposits
on the table, and announces lunch served.
Fish and chips. Their first. Fantastic.
On this tale they have dined out many times.
The Merouns' house, a sixteenth-century
salt-barn, rendered three-storey *merveilleuse*
close to the city's heart, was once attached
to an abbey or convent. They tell us, as
food appears with minimum fuss – a tart
or pie assembled from silver-foiled balls

of pastry (made on the weekend), layered
with salmon, onion, eggs and herbs – about
the princess affianced to some king, the abbey
built to compensate for breach-of-promise
when she was given to someone else instead
by her brother William the Conqueror . . .
Webs of story bear up the meal, like a
tracery tablecloth. They remember the motel
where everything on the menu is meat
and great alarm is caused when the foreigners
ask for dessert. Daniel gives us a barbecue.
It, too, seems indefinably French, though this,
they protest, is an Australian habit they have kept.
During the daytimes, we wander the streets –
one can't say, 'of old Caen' – since the city was
reduced to rubble, probably needlessly, shortly
before the Allied rescue whose birthday it is.
In Caen's city square we eat the best pizza
of the trip: *carpaccio* with a whole egg
and chili oil. Overfed foreigners, not us
especially, mostly the Rescuers, or their
children, crowd the streets. Some days, food
does seem *de trop*, especially the day we go to
the Museum, and look at pictures of the town
in '44, when every block was blitzed to shards
and our senses reel with imagined assault
the smell and colour of hot bitumen.

Wellington Wahine

sleep through a blustery night in Wellington
like weathering a storm at sea
a night crossing

in this room, two desks backed against each other
hand-decorated bookshelves, Greg and Jen's
care and pleasure in every item
boxes and stacks of organised work stuff
detail attended to, chaotic rightness

from the hotel, take the turning
at the Cloreen corner
a bowl of milk coffee at Red's
feral family and friends at Castro's
leave the baby's ball behind

crumpled copper edging on half-moon
cafe table, a scream from a passing siren
jazz clarinet over the PA, a red wall
an ochre wall, recessed lights with
perforated covers. Sunday morning copies
of *The Dominion* on every table

yesterday was Pat's anniversary
I read the poem with him in it
lots of red-Celt children about
one in a green dress twirls on a bar stool
loads of resolved-looking women
in great shoes, suit jackets, tights

the red wall has black blotches
like old telephone booths

the waitress's t-shirt says
Samoan Power: Penina Tautele
ole Pasefika. Levine's, the paint people
offered free paint for Festival art
all-weather oils for a double mural
each end of the hillside tunnel
Inferno and Paradiso, bravely but
badly rendered

Seven Cases of Domestic Violence:
a book in the Unity Bookshop, on
Maori women's experiences – though
once and future warriors, all colours,
practise at home. Big blokes stride
along the malls, bulging shoulders
rolling gait, one shouts directions
to a mate, who veers into
the Lotto office

agendas aren't fashionable, says Dinah
the poet, but she has one: calmness, oneness
with the leaves and stones, going quietly
knowing what to hold and what put down

the right holds. Yes.
the woman casts Lucifer down to Hell
stands with her foot on the serpent's neck
a nun spoke to me yesterday, and
Gregory met 'a wall of nuns'
I tell Dinah my anger, slander those
good women, who were good to her too

who scorned to be temples of delight
not down here, anyway. Tell it not,
your wrath doth grow. Even told, it
hangs around. Sisters, unite!
learn Wing Chun –
invented by a Buddhist nun
praise the Lord and
storm the houses

extra-virgin vigilantes

Base Clay

red clay disgorged by the new post-hole
gives the lie to designer topsoil

baked, dry, crumbly   it means
'home' or 'then' when our world
was young

truckloads of rich thick brown loam
sit on top of it all over the Adelaide plains
– mudpacks

that never soften the base
complexion, Bay-of-Biscay red
left to itself, it grows abundant prickles, three-

corner-jacks, paddy-melons, couch & a straggly
leguminous grass that has little pea-pods we
searched out and ate

on blasted-heath playgrounds that proliferated in
the '50s, the kind with hot-metal maypoles
rings at the end of dangling chains

circular running-tracks pounded into the dirt around
where kids trotted faster and faster, gathering momentum,
leaving the ground and whirling, arms pulled taut

a stumpy tap by the fence perhaps, no trees, a jungle-gym
death-defying swings & on the ground, patches of
those little pea-things that tasted dusty, nutty, sweet

the clay supports geraniums, lantana, succulents
stone-fruit trees if you keep the water up to them, but
lawns, even kikuyu, develop worn patches

like mangy dogs, red-brown hide showing through
The slides of Moi's and Jack's kids have Moi in a 'shift'
boys in cadet gear on the lawn

slouch hats and sergeant stripes, gaiters, boots
lined up on the bare bits outside the rumpus room
in front of the nectarines

sun-whitened palings falling down in the background
Along the walk from our place to theirs, Sturt Creek,
Marion Oval where the kids who were allowed to be

in Marching Girls raised bottle-tanned calves, swung
fists in white gloves; almond and bamboo groves on
alluvial soil near the river

by the time you got to Warradale it was all packed plains clay
sprouting a bleak block of shops, butcher deli greengrocer
push-button phone in a concrete corner bunker

& the playground, a poor second-option, the beach
if your feet lasted infinitely more alluring, another mile or
so in that same westward straight line

clay giving way finally to gorious sand and mirror-blue
healing water. Some of the bible stories we empathised with
most
were the ones where hosts welcomed travellers by

washing their feet. We did it for ourselves, standing in
friends' back yards having hiked from our place
running warm water from their hose over

making red mud

Surprisingly,

Adelaide roses are spectacular

All Day, All Night

So, Greg, going around, ever conscious of the life that gets away
as you say, do you ever find you can stare it out (life), fix it
with a gimlet eye as it

goes about its business in, say, a patch of chickweed around the
base
of a gum tree up the back of a holiday cabin, on the first
sunny day in weeks

sitting (like this) on an old tyre for an hour, feet in the grass,
Being
In It, the way they tell you to be in the 'Life, Be in It' campaigns?
worth a try

Judith tells me my book will be even later appearing. I want to
hit her,
but instead shed frustrated tears. Your Felix could be a waiter at
the launch
at this rate

You say, children's fanaticism about life amuses, and appals
(true)
but (also true) we merely get better at pretending not to care, or
only about big things

Anna cried herself to sleep a few days back over her friend Beth
whom she's known 'all my life', moving one place further up the
table
in the classroom

These hurts mount up. You may cry less, but your only reward
will likely be cancer. Now you have your children's hurts
to cry for, too

This weekend, Anna has Beth and others staying overnight
at the Grand, for her birthday, which should revive her standing.
For some reason, I recall

catching the trailing sleeve of my novice's habit on the Best Parlour door-
handle, causing me almost to drop the tray of best silver and china I'd offered
to visiting priests

(Best Guests). My novice mistress was dismayed to hear me mutter darkly
about the stupid sleeves having to be worn down, so as to be proper
this was not 'like me'

I wish I had more words to live by. I'd like to offer you 'So and so says . . . '
as you do, at apposite points, but the snatches that come to mind are random
old songs: 'All day,

all night, Maryanne,' . . . My brother Pat, who died, once rolled his car gently
down Willunga Hill, near where we're staying. It came to rest against a tree. A
brown Valiant Charger

the motorbike was more 'him'. He got done for DUI riding it home from Uni. He
left school early, eloped a t sixteen, married Laura eight years later, then they split.
He did adult Matric,

two years' Politics, but alcoholism is (as you say) in the genes.
You can say for Pat
he took his thirty-one years at a run hauling buckets of concrete
on a worksite in
that (unsuspected) last week

You write about land and being of it. The only patch I felt I
occupied was
our first backyard, with the Geraldton Wax you climbed to
Mr. Gilles' fence post

a sprawling de-facto sandpit out the back we colonised, summer
squatters,
with the tap on, making roads. So unattached now, and hardly
mystical 'detachment'

wombling free? I'm waiting, though, for what happens post-
menopause
Is this when us women (your 99–75%) get what we want? They
say our testosterone
levels start to match men's

I'm waiting to be more territorial, stroppy. There are so many
people I've
never told to bugger off. I could stack on a total wobbly, or just
sulk
the way my boss does

Has Felix found his feet by now? I like that term, 'toddler'. I was
always
so careful to keep mine on the ground, 99–75% of the time
my testo-surge will

propel me into late adventurousness, *benedictus sum in mulieribus*,
at last
Surf's up! My uncle Bob (a priest) sent me Jacques Prévert's
Paroles
in the novitiate

I've forgotten 100% of them. Who needs words when there's
deeds to
be done, in lands as yet unthought of? Ken is being an idiot,
leaping around the room

clapping his hands and declaring 'Porky Pierman!' (someone we
know)
the pursuit of wisdom? Could be. 99–75% of being an adult is
finding
ways of tricking yourself

back into the water. Bless me Father, for I have wimped out. Not
for
much longer! At this Poetry Weekend, a newly-formed troupe of
Aboriginal dancers opens proceedings

we're in the Southern Fleurieu, an hour out of town, where
rivers have
names like Yankalilla, Anacotilla, Congeratinga – for the dance,
a patch of
'land' was hastily assembled

on orange plastic over carpeted floor. These Tjilbruki Dancers
said
where they were from, then began to dance, two blokes in their
twenties,
a handful of little fellas

a hawk dance, to show sailing, hovering, swooping, grabbing
prey
one boy especially, about nine, so engrossed, so elegant, so
terrific
I was all choked up

forgot to be embarrassed at how trumped-up the occasion
seemed,
the boy was the hope of our whole mob, the Child sent to save
while elsewhere down here

at Christ Church Yankalilla, a weird revival of a moribund,
ambiguous
faith as theVirgin appears in shoddy plasterwork, bearing her
Son
thousands gather

Members of the Council for Aboriginal Reconciliation are
quitting in
protest, as the government cuts $400 million from the fund
administered
by Aboriginals themselves

it'll go from legal and cultural services, community work
projects. There
are marches in the streets again. Interesting times, dastardly
schemes
we're scraping up our rage

may malaise pass you by, as it seems to, you and Jen
and your hot grommet, every day present 'the kind of job
you could do'

and may the Lord preserve you from bush poets
whom one day I will boo

Big Kids

a childish whim, hosing down the verandah
which occasionally I do

the hose nozzle adjusted to
water-cannon whoosh

the vine-roofed brick floor dotted with
hardy potplants has its

autumn leafed-in aspect, grapes pecked clean
russet leaves sitting tight a few weeks yet

Indian summer and I'm sharing the yard
with birds, big and brutal-looking

noisy crickets, a new variety
all-day-chirp

scattered deck-chairs on the lawn
toys too, after Georgia-Rose and Clinton

found the old tar-coloured teapot
for 'bee-tend' tea

the dead gondola telephone for
pretend long-distance

two Garfield plush-toys, the little one
stuffed inside the larger

Georgia liked the lawn, and chewed
dry leaves, pointed at the pigeons

Doug's, next-door, circling the house
Clinton shook a quince from the tree

coriander's thriving, basil too, in
a warm April. I select herbs for the name

the way Mum picks horses.. germander
and veronica, Pansies Super Giant

pea-straw bought to Peter Cundall's
instructions, but the garden's too restrained

sometimes it seems plants and I have
a deep accord, but really I just fuss and

hope for the best. Not being born to it
yet nature myths are bunk –

'Born Mother' is one, the trick being
simply to be at ease, not plagued

by too much fret, but *there*, solid
if Ruth or Marg or I had waited for that

we wouldn't have a kid between us
but there they are

tough enough, cossetted in fits and starts
straggling through dry patches

when we tend our own plots, still
growing ourselves, weedily, up

I throw the quince that Clinton left
at those bloody birds,

go into the back room, my cubby while
Ken's away, to make picnic tea

in his cockroach cup

View from the Pier

Reading Robert Dessaix
I muse on how well
men tell stories

hands to the wheel
eyes on the main
narrative drag

or metaphysical drift

they can see a life
(an own life, even)
as if it were a ship

on the point of disappearing
over the horizon, perhaps
but whose wake is

still clearly visible
miraculously holding a shape,
only frothing and bubbling

a little, on gentle seas

sharply defined
years after launch-date

    the course so far
    clearly navigable

The boys stand on their
separate piers, astrolabes
and compasses at hand

mapping their trajectories

tracing elegant intersections
and parallels, sketching in
the most adroit of

marginal illustrations and

charming *divagations*
yet the contours of the map
the shape of the life

a life worthy of a big 'L'
stay fast, hold good,
stand out in bold relief

    needing only to be coloured in

(Kate Jennings, in
Bad Manners, says
we mustn't say 'boys'
shocked that we're rude
in quite that way)

girls tell shreds of tales
only ask for bits
'... how's your Mum? Since the

doctor's news?' 'Not bad,
bit flat, ask again
next week ... '

up to our knees in
threads come loose
the view an endless ocean

of woolly tales un-
ravelling, skeins
of our lives

My sister says

'I'm back on the path, I think'
or 'that seems to have blown
over'

I see us being dragged
at a great speed, many with
our eyes closed,

somewhere, we understand that,
it's just not safe to
look quite yet

and if you try to
look back, the wind's
in your eyes,

and anyway you've got
a kid under each arm
is this a ski slope?

it's not a cruise

a course, possibly,
in the sense of assault-course

no plot to speak of

we seem to be
along for the ride

Note

Robert Dessaix's book is *A Mother's Disgrace*

Which Haze?

In Europe there is
usually, in summer,
sun behind haze

illuminating you at your cafe table
dusting a soft glaze over your bit of touristing

par exemple in Normandy, in Caen
(rebuilt from rubble)
wandering in quite considerable
heat down sheltered alleys
or along canals

with such a sun observing

you wondering how you strike the locals
knowing (really) they would need to
be dying of terminal *ennui*

before *une étrangère* impinged
du tout

back in Oz you try occasionally on indeterminate,
unseasonal, hot late autumn days like this
to recreate the feel of there

but can't avoid being more comfortable, more
genuinely cosmopolitan (true)

than one was ever able to be
là-bas, even with passable *français*

here you can choose at leisure
a cafe, for its *soi-disant* European feel

trade pleasantries and mild
flirtatiousness *à la mode* with waiters
knowing without thinking comment *ça se fait ici*

that this steel-topped round table
half-empty wine-glass
café crème (cappuccino, actually)

sheltered by this Fosters Special brolly
and on which you also rest your novel on this
no-work day

can carry all the meanings, real and fictional
you care to lay upon it

while that mythical, if in some bang-your-shin-on-me manner
real
one you sat at in Paris or Caen wasn't yours, really, to rest
meanings on

could barely wait (*en effet*)
to shrug you off with your
ten-a-penny postcards, change-purse
bière à pression, sunglasses and stamps

to send you on your way with a Gallic
pout, a '*ben alors* (pfaugh!)'

aware (without caring) that you'll be
happier *chez toi*

here in this cafe where the food is genuinely terrif.
and worth a trip, at least across town
ambience seriously chic, not up itself
not yet an open secret in this town composed of them

where you can remember tiny triumphs
over there

hum the Marseillaise quietly to yourself

say *au revoir* to the frisky waiter and mean it

Way off among the cars . . .

light on mottled brick, the glow on
timber around doors and windows where there's
        lacquer left to reflect sun

    next-door's lawn-mower / old electric-cord type
    with a roller, its burr of sound making you think of
    bowling greens, lawns like carpet, sedate pursuits

a pair of rubber boots, black with blue soles and cuffs leaning at
the angle where the wall turns a corner; down that side
if I turn my head will be white quince-blossom, wisteria

    all these tug at me, my heart (recovering from flu
     inclining to detect harmonies

    the clutch of paint tins on the yellow kindy-table
      signing a household keen to Keep Itself Nice rather than
one that doesn't put things away

& Janet Charman's 'dad driving . . . ' /
                                        country Show (NZ)
poem,   despite a chill behind the word 'perfect'
                                                    repeated

        calls up Easter Weekend races, Mallala
        & echoes of Irish Dancing contests, miles
        out of town, dad driving,   not

Maryborough, Myponga
                                        Macclesfield ? (yes)

us high-stepping, arms by sides,
 shuddering platforms
raising dust in summer paddocks

        medals still in our mother's wardrobe drawers

I reach her end-line: 'where is our brother'

so, as I must, I
pencil him in

– chasing up the hill after our cousins to
our vantage points for the Great Eastern
some horses down every time in the steeplechase

we aren't always watching

This novel, also – 1988 –

boys careering towards some Great Excess,
asks
me, us impertinent
about our brother, late / where he is

well, 'way off among the cars' (Janet knows)

despite it being true that
six, skinny, gap-toothed, all those
mornings with

(us) his sisters he ran behind Mr Allen's
milk-truck, the horizon close as the
Dusty Track turnoff

a white linen suit for marrying in, a white caravan
washed downstream / at this point we can't help
seeing portents / or reading them, backwards

Irish

instead, ladies

take your place in this commodious square of order

as it may be the front seat of the car on a calm day

humming a reel or a jig
the two big girls, maybe one or two smaller
our pumps black and soft our socks too white to be true

dad

driving

Sense and Sensibility

Peppery smell in the backyard
scant sun on the back of my neck
familiar call of a bird   from all sides
that I can't identify

Easter Monday in a year when
Good Friday was Family Fun Day
at the Showgrounds   and Jane Austen
has risen from the dead

Austen mania all over the English-speaking
world: BBC series, film versions of the novels
strange comfort to be derived from
her resurrection

albeit the tales are all of little pigs to market
happy ending (only ending)   the bill of sale
stamped with his seal by Mr Bennett
                    Mr Elliot or whomever

On Easter Sunday Mum unearths a document
with similar flavour   from 1966
John Grey Gorton (Federal minister-in-charge
of Education)   writes to my father

informing him with pleasure that his daughter
Catherine has won a Commonwealth scholarship
to cover her final two years' schooling

                                        sharing with him the hope
she will attain the promise revealed by her winning
the award.
                              It's nothing like irritation I feel when
I see the letter

    dismay – realising how he was encouraged

on all sides
to see us

his five daughters, a latter-day Mr Bennett
unaware of the imminent days of ferment,
the forthcoming diaspora,
to see us

as his responsibility
when any moment we'd be off like firecrackers

Catherine-wheels spinning out of sight
leaving him, unconsidered, behind

he never walked a single one of us down any aisle
when he would have shone in the role

we gave him unchurched grandchildren

'Plant one!' he'd say, indicating a cheek
they mobbed him every time

Victoria's Secret

the way a shining body of water seems to sit

just a little above the field, as you drive

towards it, in the country

the way the shimmery lady looked to Bernadette

and her little cousins, by that rocky creek

in Portugal, beautiful but indistinct

is the way the perfect clothes for you

appear eternally to your mind's eye, softly

incandescent, shadowy, just about to take shape

beckoning you on through life

The Walk

Check ahead
for
small
distant
figure in
dark colours
ronding
the corner
not yet
amble up
our street
winter sun
Lorna (per
haps) is out.
Her
front yard
pin-neat
flanking
Pratt's place
dark & overgrown
Mrs P.
wig under scarf
bikes off into
any weather
sturdy, sound
as
bicycle bells
Houses curtained
clipped
decent
except the flats
sign sometimes
outside:
'Palms Read'

once a baby
nappy trailing
wandered
house
to
house
lost all day
Dad, it turned
out, sleeping
in there

            I meet
Anna, now
from the bus
since
she was
one day
followed

        The
boy, though
we've deduced
lives
(probably)
hereabouts
brother of Jessica
(maybe)

This straight
north-south
line
most afternoons
I
walk it

hold
my breath
till she
appears
tiny
in
the distance

Local History

Hard rubbish collection day
The One Day of the Year
for hardened collectors
like me (scavenging at seven)
true, our Council ward
still has its leavening of battlers
you get a better class of rubbish
over Goodwood Road, in West-
bourne and Hyde Parks
Our household's roadside pile
Is real junk, rustic, years-in-the
-garden lichened, rusted, rained-on
or bug-eaten away to a uniform earth colour
the bark that fell away from
the shadehouse palings
the left-in-the-weather-deckchairs
(still sporting some mottled yellow)
the two guinea pig cages
the smaller homemade and
the scavenged one – so capacious
Mo always looked lost in it
now Mo's lost too, so out it goes
rusted bike frames and assorted
parts (some slivers of purple paint)
a cracked fish tank that once held
mice – Molly and Hermione – another
sad tale (H quite happy as a solitary
till we felt compelled to introduce M
who exercised to death, followed prompt-
ly by her terminally-shocked friend)
icons of good intentions, all
the healthy, outdoor, include-our-
furry-friends urges
This afternoon, the land Rovers
cruise by, one after another
I sit in the front yard, on a

garden seat acquired on just
such a day, and listen contentedly
as the purring engines growl softer
on the other side of the wall
then roar away unsated
Meanwhile, I hear Terry over the road
carting his surely flawless castoffs
gutterwards. I wait till the shuffling stops
wait some more, then nip across
and purloin a slide-back recliner
(60s), which joins two bijou
ironwork tables (need work, great
bones), two more garden chairs
and a fabulous pink, white and gold
Tammy-era girls' dressing table.
Heaven will be endless days like this
with just enough space between
to grow greedy again

King of Sturt Creek

It's 1962, or thereabouts
Some gallant Visionary of Commerce
owner of the South Road Neptune Service
Station, erects a six-foot concrete
Neptune, cresting a sweep of lawn on the
Sturt Creek embankment. The King stands
in a shallow basin, white, strong, upright
if rudimentary of form, grasping his iron
trident, from which three jets of water spit
he's wearing an iron crown
He marked the place along the creek
where we liked to end our walks
stared impassively across the constant flow
of cars, across the valley of vineyards
to his lost kingdom on the horizon
Most times we passed him by without
attending to what, perhaps, he stood for
In a short span of human time, the ravages
of his own element reshaped the royal features
rust-tears at first, then more corrosive
channelling, exposing iron bones.
We never thought to wonder, why this god?
Neptune, Poseidon, monarch of the sea
beneath which runs the blacker tide
bearing us on towards the new Atlantis
He got sadder, stranded there, knee-deep
in weed and stagnant damp, and stumped off,
finally, I guess, disgusted, as the eighties dawned
no room for kings or deeps of any kind
perhaps to pass the word to Midas that
an opening had come up
which he might care to fill

Ki Ki

An old man in a baseball cap
hunched over outside the Grosvenor
    hands across his crotch

I'd like to say something
redemptive, fantastical and salutary here
    but I can't, all he looks is sad

from my satchel, a breast, two breasts
peek above the other papers
    Annie Sprinkle's, displayed by the owner

with a cheesy, cheerleader's grin
she has painted them as the two halves
    of the yin/yang symbol

why can't I work up any interest
in her performance art
    Is the cervix really beautiful?

It's Friday and I've just spoken to
Iris Frame, who's not post-anything
    though she's certainly 81

In the gallery, amidst her 'ki-ki' paintings
invented bush creatures, naive to the max
    how to begin marking her place

    in the 'panoply of feminism'?

For John Forbes
1950–1998

ex tuis litteris cognovi cursus navigationum tuarum
(CICERO)

Day after Valentine's Day
    empty couch across the room
sombre Celtic drums from Shooglenifty

You could tell me who Saint Valentine was . . .
    a Roman martyr?   Feb. 14 in
my calendar now is the day Pat died

I told you about Pat – off like a rocket
    at thirty-one (what's more, you
remembered)   'You were right

about all that Catholic stuff, mate' –
    it had more power to define us
forever than we cared to allow

You stood at the end of that table there
    inclined at that alarming forward angle
declaiming 'Total Fucking Gas' to Gabe

inscribed your poems for him
    with summary eschatology: 'be a spanner
in the works of death'

on the couch, and ill, chastened on a wet
    November night, you talked about
your dad & mum, whom I didn't expect

to meet so soon.   At your send-off
    St John Bosco's, Engadine
the de la Salles reached out to claim you

via the *mitteleurop* celebrant, in a service
    I thought you'd loathe, then thought
you wouldn't, the triteness would evaporate

from your vantage point in the gods
    you'd see stricken us, hear the word 'poet'
repeated often, think – 'fair enough'

morning poem

I get up and read
some Jim Schuyler
a Ken thing to do

and Jim makes me feel
        confirmed
in the sorts of things I notice

in the morning
        when there's time

that's what strikes me
        in his poems is

how leisured they seem

and then I iron
my Sally Bluff georgette
shirt, my Sally Bluff
linen pants

in a spirit Schuyler
would approve

admiring the cut, the
make, the hang, the
'stuff'

the top cut like a
herald's, or page-boy's

if you can imagine
a page in
white georgette

– Jim could –
fitting sleeves
flared at the cuffs

double-layered tunic
nearly see-through
even so

voile is what it's like
a word in two
Schuyler poems
I read just now

one to tell
Darragh Park –
who did his
book-cover –

(feathery green-gold bushes
flowers in pink and purple
spears and splotches)

– that *voile et vapeur*
is Paris slang for bisexual

did Jim know the phrase
'batting for the other team'

and do we, in our
vernacular, extend that
to 'batting for both teams'?

come to that, though,
the French would be 'sail
and steam', not our 'voile'

but voile, yes, for
this georgette. It feels
like some vestal garment

and there are days
when it wouldn't
be the right choice

the pants are linen
so fine they float

loose, straight, soft,
white with bands of
grey-and-white

I wear them together
hand-washed last night
hung to dry in the shower

'Who/needs
a costly tweed suit?' asks
James . . . and answers himself

'I can't say I need one, but

I sure would like one'
He's in love with Tom
(secretary). I can't say I
need a secretary, but I

sure would like one

it's Sunday, still and hot
a Hitchcock-type bird
brown, heavy, mean

the ones that scuffle

threateningly in dry leaves
sits on the garden seat
discarded by people in a
big house, next suburb up

reclaimed and repainted white

I slept heavily
rather than well
and now my eyes ache

the greens in the yard all soft
the house-front pinky-yellow
sandstone

James sits at a dining table
'staring out at a dark pink
weigela' (it's) 'going over'
?

James gets calmer all the time
Thorazine

swim next, ignore the birds
sit by the herbs
calme et volupté

the whippersnipper stops
breathy stillness returns
soft sun in patches

no secretary but
a white damask quilt
on my bed

Trip

slurred blues in the car

                                        sounds like 'blue hippy town'
'Chicago' – pretty sure –

Go West, young man
I think –

the slurring blurs with
how this bug's affecting me
          dizzy, stoned

only kind of stone these days

80 k's to the Folk Fest
half a tank

                                        but the car revs too high
even coasting downhill

doped-out, meander through
my live broadcast, interviews
in low gear, the laid-back ideal
          hard to achieve, *compos*, easy now

winding home, afternoon
westering home with a song in the air
blues in stereo fade in and out

hey everybody, let little Junior know
somebody hoodoo'd the
hoodoo man

watch your step, Junior – be good
see that Long Day Care & Early Learning Centre?
you wouldn't like it

I pass Celtic Avenue where
the Haines's house was: Mal and Val
and their five babushka dolls
bandbox daughters with silky bangs

a house where everyone washed
her own plate, and Val
sewed all their dresses

meet me in the bottom
tell me who's that peepin'
in my window?

can't quite make out the face
go away, I'm sick

on the hillside, over Willunga Hill
          the sun suddenly breaks through
                         too-green grass leans away from me
a slick of light coating the blades

cars accumulate behind but I'm
          sticking to ninety

while, magic-lanterned across the windscreen,
the Folkie parade trots past again, no-one I know
          impeccably fresh, middlingly smudged
or no-turning-back faces

I remember Longford, Tasmania
too cold for frivolity

today was cold and wet as well
hand-woven jumpers for folk blokes
kids in daggy layers, not city grunge
        pelts and hats and leggings
                no Kramer shirts

zip, zip, you give me that buzz

they came for Margaret Roadknight, eight feet tall
she sang once with the Melbourne
Short Women's Choir in
Castlemaine Town Hall

and there was Bert Jansch
Pentangle, Basket of Light
two bags full of

lost innocence, or unconnectedness
before you threw in your lot with
the first wrong someone

more folkies eating junk food now

just want you to hold me, baby
and let the music carry on
baby on moonshine, whooee

remember when the word 'debonair'
was still used in commercials?
it's 'de bon air', anglicised
never thought of that before
write it down

please take a walk with me sometime,
come on, what can I do, I did
everything I could
must be muskets (?) I found

Harmers Haven

the washing-machine needs
a new agitator

my sister needs a new heart-valve
choice of metal or pigskin

in order that agitation can go on

producing the cardiac chorale –
sigh, pulse, thrum, push, pause

no arrest being made at this stage
at some later date, absolutely

I sit on the sand at Wonthaggi
with Ros

in the nick since
no one's around

the kids play in bathers

a lot of my time with Ros has been
sans clothes
on
summer days
across a swag of years

before the girls
(pounding off now
with a blow-up seal
into the dunes)
unclad

in long grass or,
when *en ville*, on concrete

There's Julie
bending over tomatoes or basil
out the back of Florence Street
pink and white and luminous

Ros and me on the cement
like chops on a barbie

our faith in the sun-god, those days, unshaken

this day, now, we've brought three lots of sunscreen
the girls trot back to be re-coated

while a hollow ache where time has drained
like dishwater
lodges dully underneath my ribs

children and beach-house
shining, precious, hard-won
no fair exchange

Helene with MS, twisted and strong at my swimming-pool
took swimming classes at the beach 'out there all
day with only a visor'
bends columnar mahogany-tanned
legs

sings doughtily under her breath for all the interminable time
it takes to dress herself

Ros is looking forward
to menopause –

I say I am but I'm not
I want to stay among
the green and fertile
in the pink like Julie

Cross two fingers in front of my face
against the onset of the sere
and sallow years

try to soak up wholeness
from the sand & salt

Steve Kelen has a poem which says
You are the beach, you are the beach

we never say 'the seaside' or 'the sea'
– 'the beach', 'the water' –

we took our babies to Maslin's in their bassinettes
a surf baptism for longevity

under the cold Bass Strait water we hear the
world's pulse

surely there'll be desolation
when our blood-tides
won't respond,
moon-wounds dry up

In the morning Ros
fishes from the rocks

the backs of my legs are burnt

the girls, sea-monkeys,

scramble out of the Deep Pool

we are the beach

we drag it with
us

into the car

it doesn't die till 10 k.s out of Melbourne

Printed in the United Kingdom
by Lightning Source UK Ltd.
9533400001B

9 781876 857097